ALL YOU
WANT FOR
CHRISTMAS

ALL YOU WANT FOR CHRISTMAS

DAVID PLATT

10 Publishing
a division of 10 of those.com

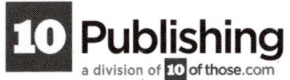

British Library Cataloguing in Publication Data
A record for this book is available from the British Library

ISBN: 978-1-83728-069-8

Designed by Jude May
Cover image © dar woto | iStock
Printed in India

10Publishing, a division of 10ofthose.com
6b Upper Water Street, Newry, Co Down, Northern Ireland, BT34 1DJ
info@10ofthose.com
www.10ofthose.com

1 3 5 7 10 8 6 4 2

For family members, friends, and others
who don't yet know the Servant of our souls

Contents

Contents

Introduction

Why did
Jesus come?

Introduction

Why did Jesus come?

What do you want for Christmas?

As a dad of six kids ranging in age from eighteen down to two, this question evokes a variety of responses in my home. And a variety of price tags, as well. My two-year-old's request for a car is a lot easier to fulfill than my eighteen-year-old's request for the same!

I wonder how *you* might respond to this question. In fact, I want to ask you to pause for a moment and actually answer it. If you could receive anything for Christmas, what would it be?

Your first thought may be a particular possession, but I'd encourage you to go a bit deeper than that. For example, in recent years, there have been challenges in my life, my family, and my work, and I've found myself just wanting rest. Or peace. Or strength. Or healing for people I love who are hurting. I've wanted hope that there's some light at the end of the tunnel.

I'm guessing I'm not alone. At the deepest level, we all want our needs met and our desires fulfilled. And I think if we're honest, we would love the idea of someone coming to us, asking us what we want for Christmas, and then providing that very thing.

> The heart of Christmas is actually about receiving what you most want

Now what if I told you that the heart of Christmas is actually about receiving what you most want and need?

I'm guessing you may be skeptical. After all, the events of the first Christmas—Jesus' birth in Bethlehem surrounded by angels and shepherds—seem far removed from the desires or needs you and I may have in the twenty-first century. And we're quite used to advertisements over-promising and under-delivering, especially at this time of year.

But what if this is really true? Despite the understandable doubts you may have about the Christmas story or its relevance for your life, I'd like to ask you to read the pages ahead with an open mind and heart. In this short book, I want to share with you four reasons why Jesus came. As I do, I invite you to at least imagine what it would be like if there was one true God who loves you so much that he wants to *give to* you, rather than *take from* you.

> God loves you so much that he wants to *give to* you, rather than *take from* you

What if the Christmas story is actually about how the God who made you wants to fulfill your deepest longings and meet your deepest needs?

Imagine what that gift would mean for you not just this Christmas or this coming year, but forever.

Reason 1

To be
with you

Reason 1

To be with you

… the Son of Man came …

Journey with me to a temple in Southeast Asia. I remember sitting at a table on the green grass of the temple grounds, looking up at the multi-tiered brown pagoda beside. Two religious leaders sat with me, one of them Buddhist and the other Hindu.

For a while, our conversation revolved around simply getting to know one another, learning about each other's lives and families. Eventually, our conversation shifted to faith. We talked about beliefs we shared with one another, including the need to love and respect other people and work for the good of all. Then one of them made the following statement.

"We may have different views about small issues, but when it comes down to the most important issues, our religions are the same."

The other leader nodded with a smile, then asked me what I thought.

I paused for a moment, then I said, "It sounds as though you both picture God (or whatever you may call 'god') at the top of a mountain while we're all standing at the bottom. I may take one path up the mountain while you may take another, but in the end we will all be in the same place."

At this point, they were both smiling and nodding. One of the men replied happily, "Exactly, you understand!"

Then I paused for another moment, leaned in, and said, "I have a question: What would you think if I told you that the God at the top of the mountain actually came down to where we are? What if God doesn't wait for us to find our way to him, but instead comes to us?"

They thought for a moment and then both responded. "That would be great."

I replied, "Let me introduce you to the fundamental difference between our beliefs: Jesus."

This picture—of God coming to be with us—is at the heart of Christmas. Over and above all the wonderful traditions you or I may be accustomed to at Christmastime, from singing carols to swapping gifts to sharing meals with family and friends, Christmas is a revolutionary, radical, mind-blowing, earth-shaking claim that God himself has come to be with us. When an angel told Joseph about Jesus' birth, that's exactly what

> God coming to be with us is at the heart of Christmas

he declared: Jesus would be called "Immanuel," which means "God with us" (Matthew 1:23).

So why did God come to be with us in Jesus? Well, the Bible lists a multitude of reasons why he entered our world. Here is a quick sampling:

Jesus came to make a way for us to have abundant, eternal life.
(John 3:16; 10:10)

Jesus came to seek those who've lost their way and help those who don't have it all figured out.
(Luke 19:10; Mark 2:17)

Jesus came to bring light in a dark world and redeem what is broken.
(John 12:46; Galatians 4:4–5)

Jesus came to take away sins and free people from the fear of death.
(1 John 3:5; Hebrews 2:14–15)

Yet out of all the verses in the Bible that talk about why Jesus came, one in particular has always stood out to me. In a sense, this specific verse summarizes all the others, but it also takes things to another level—a level that is, frankly, shocking. It almost feels inappropriate to say, and I wouldn't believe it if it didn't come straight from the mouth of Jesus himself:

> *"For even the Son of Man came not to be served but to serve, and to give his life as a ransom for many."*
> *(Mark 10:45)*

This one verse depicts all four of the reasons I want to show you about why Jesus was born in Bethlehem 2,000 years ago, and it highlights this first reason—that Jesus came to be with you and me—in a brilliant way.

Think about Jesus' words in this statement. We can almost miss their significance if we're not careful, but did you notice that Jesus is the only person ever born who can say that he decided to be born? "The Son of Man *came* …"

No one else in all of history has made that decision. None of us concluded one day, "I think it's about time *to come* to the world." That's because, of course, none of us existed before we were conceived.

But Jesus did.

This is part of the mystery of Christmas. The Bible refers to Jesus as the Son of God. This description of Jesus is often misunderstood (and sometimes intentionally misrepresented) because Jesus is not God's Son in the same way I am my father's son. God didn't have a relationship with Mary that produced Jesus like my parents had a relationship with one another that produced me.

The Bible uses the word "son" in many ways beyond merely describing a male born to parents. For example, at times "son" can simply refer to someone's nature or identity, and that's how "son" is used to refer to Jesus. These two titles for Jesus—*Son of Man* and *Son of God*—specifically point us to Jesus' human nature and divine nature. The title Son of Man highlights how Jesus is fully human (like us). The other title, Son of God, emphasizes how Jesus is fully divine (unlike us). And when you put these two titles together, you realize what makes Jesus different from every other person in the history of the world: he is God in the flesh.

That's how Jesus could decide to come into the world, and it makes the story of Christmas the most amazing news in the world. For Christmas is an extraordinary declaration that God is not a distant deity separated from us and all the hurts and heartaches, challenges and struggles we experience in this world of evil and suffering. Instead, God has come to be with us, to meet us where we are, and to make a way for us to have life with him.

This is so important to understand in a world where many people think that all religions are fundamentally the same, and that any differences between beliefs are merely superficial. Often people say, in a similar way to the sentiments expressed by my friends outside that Southeast Asian temple, "Just choose whichever religion works best for you—or no religion at all—because all of our paths are essentially alike."

But Christmas tells us that's not true. The utterly unique message of Christmas is that God has come to be with us! No other religion makes that claim.

> The utterly unique message of Christmas is that God has come to be with us—no other religion makes that claim

And think about *why* God came to be with us. It feels almost too obvious to write, but I want to make sure you don't miss it: God *came* to be with us because apparently, God *wants* to be with us.

———————

A friend of mine was telling me about a conversation he'd had with a man who was extremely wealthy, attractive, successful, and overly confident in himself. My friend asked him, "Do you think you will go to heaven when you die?"

The man pondered for a moment, then said, "Yes, I believe I will go to heaven."

"Why do you think that?" my friend asked.

"Because I believe God wants me there."

When I heard this story, I immediately thought, "What an arrogant man!" But then, after further reflection, I realized he's right. God does want him there. And he wants me there, too. And you, as well! Not because you're rich, attractive, successful, or anything else in this world. Actually, not because of anything *in* you at all. He wants you there because of his great love for you. And because of his love, he wants your company forever.

I encourage you to let this soak in before moving on. God himself—the God who spoke and all creation came into being, the God who causes the sun to rise and calls the stars by name, the God before whom mountains quake and seas roar, the God who rules and reigns over all things in all the universe—came to earth as a baby because he wants to be with *you*. The God who made you and knows what is best for you loves you personally and wants you to experience abundant, eternal life with him. But there's a barrier to you and me experiencing life in relationship with God, which leads us to the second reason Jesus came.

Reason 2

To die instead of you

Reason 2

To die instead of you

... to give his life as a ransom ...

Death is not a topic we like to think much about, and for good reason. As I write these words approaching Christmas, I'm also in the midst of preparing to speak at a funeral for a man I knew all my life as Mr. Lussi. He worked as a janitor for decades but became so much more than that to the students in school and those at church like me who he would constantly encourage. Whenever anyone would ask Mr. Lussi how he was doing, no matter what was going on in his life, his reply would be the same: "I'm blessed."

I am convinced Mr. Lussi was one of the most joyful people to ever walk on this planet, and his family and friends (of whom I am grateful to be one) miss him deeply as we mourn his death.

For each of us in our lives, death is an unavoidable outcome that we try to evade. Many people dread or are even terrified of death. But this is another way Jesus is totally different from us. Death is actually the reason he came to the world. He said, "the Son of Man came … to give his life …" Somewhat strangely, this makes Christmas a celebration of a person who was born for the purpose of dying.

This difference in Jesus is even more

> Somewhat strangely, this makes Christmas a celebration of a person who was born for the purpose of dying

dramatic when you compare him with other religious leaders in history. The focus in other world religions is on a leader's life and teachings. But whether it was Muhammad dying at 62, Confucius at 72, the Buddha at 80, or Moses dying at 120 years old, for each, death marked the end of their mission.

Yet with Jesus, the opposite is true. Throughout his life, Jesus was constantly talking about, anticipating, and even foretelling his death. For the last 2,000 years, the central symbol of Christianity has been a cross—a picture of execution. The death of Jesus on the cross was not an accident; it was his plan all along, even before he was born. This little baby lying in a manger came to be nailed to a cross.

But why was it so important for Jesus to die? The answer to that question comes in what Jesus says next. He came to give his life *"as a ransom for many."* This word "ransom" refers to a payment given to release someone from slavery.

This is where *we* come into the Christmas story. God made you and me to experience full, abundant life forever in a relationship with him. The problem is, collectively and individually we have turned aside from God and his ways. The Bible calls this sin, and we are slaves to it. Left to ourselves, we all think we know better than God what is best for our lives. Every day, every one of us is prone to choose our ways over God's ways.

Just think about how this is evident even (or especially) at Christmastime. Amidst all the good tidings, Christmas crowds can quickly cause our patience to wane or our tempers to rise. Gift giving and receiving can easily turn into an endless materialistic quest for more, newer, nicer, and better possessions. Even our time with family and friends can be marked by hurt, bitterness, unforgiveness, or unresolved tensions between each other. And we observe all of the above and more on a global scale as our newsfeeds abound with headlines of evil, injustice, conflict, and war.

The world around us is full of suffering and brokenness for one reason: we are all separated from God by our sin against him. In addition, this is why we will all die. Death is the penalty for sin in each of our lives. And if we die in this state of separation from God, we will spend eternity apart from him and his love.

But this is why Jesus came: to give his life as a ransom for us. In other words, Jesus came to pay the price for our sin so that we could be free from its power and penalty in our lives: "the Son of Man came … to give his life as a ransom *for* many." The word "for" is crucial; it means "instead of."

You see, Jesus came to the world and he never sinned, not even once. As a child, he never disobeyed his parents. As a teenager, he never compromised his purity. As an adult, every word he spoke was kind, every action he took was right, and every interaction he had was loving.

His every thought, desire, and deed was just, merciful, and good.

Death is the penalty our sin deserves, but Jesus had no sin for which to die. His sinlessness is what makes him uniquely able to pay the price for our sins. After all, everyone else in the world has sinned against God, which means everyone else in the world deserves to die and is therefore not qualified to pay the price for our sins. But Jesus is, and that's why he came: to die *instead of* you. As God in the flesh, Jesus is fully able to identify with you and me in our humanity and fully able to bear divine judgment because of his deity. Jesus alone is able to take away your sin and my sin.

Early one morning, I was riding in an Uber with a driver from the Middle East named Hasim. Hasim asked me what I do for a living. As soon as I told him I was a pastor, his eyes lit up in the rearview mirror. "I can't believe this," he said. "I must tell you a story."

He began, "As a Muslim, we believe that Jesus was a prophet, but not God in the flesh. We believe it is blasphemous to think that God would become a baby. But one night I had a dream, and I saw a tiny baby who was speaking to me as clearly as an adult speaks. The baby looked directly at me and said, 'Do not question or underestimate what God can do.'" Then Hasim asked me, "Do you know what this dream means?"

"Hasim, I don't normally claim to be a dream interpreter," I replied, "but I know exactly what this one means." I continued, "God loves you so much that he has done the unthinkable. God has come to this world—to you and to me—to die on a cross for our sins." Even as I was saying those words, I knew that Muslims deny that Jesus died on a cross, but I kept going. "Jesus is God in the flesh, and he has died on the cross to make it possible for you to be forgiven of your sins and to be restored to relationship with God."

Tears welled up in Hasim's eyes, and he apologized as he wiped his face. I assured him no apologies were necessary—as long as he kept his eyes on the road!

We continued talking until it was time for me to get out of the car, at which point I asked, "Do you believe this, Hasim? Do you believe that Jesus is God in the flesh who loves you so much he came to die for your sins?"

He looked back at me and said, "Yes, this is the greatest news in the world. I absolutely believe this."

Jesus dying for us is amazingly good news but, unbelievably, it gets even better. Three days after dying, Jesus rose from the grave. Jesus lived the perfect life none of us could live, then he died the death for sin that all of us deserve to die, and ultimately he conquered the enemy none of us could conquer: death itself. He's alive! Jesus did all of this for us.

The Canadian scientist G.B. Hardy said it well:

"I checked the tomb of Buddha, and it was occupied, and I checked the tomb of Confucius and it was occupied, and I checked the tomb of Muhammed and it was occupied, and I came to the tomb of Jesus and it was empty. And I said, 'There is one who conquered death … [But] did he make a way for me to do it?' And I opened the Bible and discovered that he said, 'Because I live, you shall live also.'"

Jesus came, lived, died, and rose from the grave so that, no matter who you are or what you have done, if you will turn from your sin and trust in Jesus with your life, you can be forgiven of all your wrongdoing and restored to relationship with God forever.

Here's how Jesus put it in the most well-known verse in the Bible:

"For God so loved the world, that he gave his only Son, that whoever believes in him should not perish but have eternal life." (John 3:16)

Jesus came to die instead of you so that you can be free from the power and penalty of sin in your life forever

You are part of the world, and so I invite you to put your name in the sentence above. God so loves *you* that he gave his only Son for *you*, so that when *you* believe in Jesus, *you* will not experience eternal death, but *you* will experience eternal life in relationship with God.

Talk about a Christmas gift! Jesus came to die instead of you so that you can be free from the power and penalty of sin in your life forever.

Remember Mr. Lussi? He, like you and me, had all kinds of needs in his life: physical, mental, emotional, and relational needs. And he knew that as long as he was in this fallen world filled with sin, some of those needs would be unmet. But he also knew that Jesus had come to meet his deepest need for forgiveness and restoration to relationship with God. As a result, he knew that no matter what happened in his life or eventually in his death, he would one day have every single one of his needs perfectly met and every single one of his desires perfectly satisfied in the presence of God himself—free from sin and all of its effects for all of eternity.

And the beauty of Christmas is that this reality doesn't just change our eternity; it can also change our lives today. That's the third reason Jesus came.

Reason 3

To show you
how to live

Reason 3

To show you how to live

... not to be served ...

One of our favorite family Christmas traditions revolves around what we call "giving jars." Throughout December, our kids earn money from my wife and me for doing random acts of service around the house or in our community. Whenever they do extra chores or acts of kindness for someone else, we will give them money to put in their giving jar. They might, for example, get a small amount of money for cleaning the dishes, or a larger amount for cleaning the house! Throughout the month, these giving jars turn into quite the competition as everyone is working to have the most money in their jar. Extended family members join in the fun as well, sending money for the kids' giving jars in place of gifts for them.

When we finally come to Christmas morning, we gather around to read the Christmas story and pray. Then we pull out everyone's giving jar, and each child counts the money they've earned. Then we combine all of that money together and go "shopping" for ways to give to people in need through ministries our family supports. I remember the first time we bought a goat for a family in an impoverished country. My youngest son at the time was so excited because he thought we were buying a goat for him. When we told him it was for someone else, he was initially let down, but he's since grown to grasp the whole point of a *giving* jar!

Our Christmas tradition intentionally relates to the third reason Jesus came: to show us how to live. When you look at the scene into which Jesus spoke Mark 10:45, you realize his followers were debating about who among them was the greatest. Instead of competing about how they could out-serve each other, they were all about increasing their standing over each other. This scene mirrors the cut-throat competition we experience in a world where it seems we can't help but to constantly compare ourselves with others and promote our own interests at the expense of those around us. Jesus' followers all wanted to climb the ladder of success in this world.

Yet in his response, Jesus shatters their definition of success. Listen to the words Jesus speaks right before he explains why he came:

"And Jesus called them to him and said to them, 'You know that those who are considered rulers of the Gentiles lord it over them, and their great ones exercise authority over them. But it shall not be so among you. But whoever would be great among you must be your servant, and whoever would be first among you must be slave of all. For even the Son of Man came not to be served but to serve, and to give his life as a ransom for many.'" (Mark 10:42–45)

With these words, Jesus redefines greatness around being a servant of others. Instead of asserting yourself over others, Jesus says, "Sacrifice yourself for others." And just to make sure they (and we) understand what he means, Jesus says,

> Jesus redefines greatness around being a servant of others

"Look at those around you and see yourself as their slave."

To be clear, Jesus isn't advocating for slavery in the sense of forced servitude. Instead, this is Jesus inviting us to experience the good life (or to employ the language Jesus uses, the *great* life) by willingly laying down our lives in love for others. And as we've already seen, Jesus modeled this kind of life by giving up the glories of heaven and coming to earth to lay down his life for us.

Now we're beginning to understand how Christmas transforms not only our eternity but also our everyday priorities.

———

Picture for a moment the faces of people in your life and what it would look like for them to live to serve you. Imagine a workplace where your employer offers to work over the holidays so that you can have time off with your family or friends. Imagine a friend you don't even know very well giving you a Christmas gift with no expectation or even desire for anything in return. Imagine a family member serving you in an extravagant or unexpected way so you can have some extra rest amidst the busyness of the Christmas season.

Then realize: this is the kind of love Jesus is inviting you to show the people in your life. How might that change your posture toward family members, friends, co-workers, or classmates this Christmas season—to see yourself as their servant? And how might this change your perspective on people in need that you don't even know?

We live in a world of lonely people in need of family, of refugees in need of homes, of the enslaved in need of freedom, and of the poor and oppressed in need of provision and justice. Christmas is a call from Jesus to serve people who may not have someone else to serve them.

I have in front of me a letter from a student I'll call Cameron who recently aged out of the foster care system with no family to support him. Cameron was sleeping in train stations or parks because he had no place to go. A couple from our church, Peter and Lauren, heard about Cameron's needs, and within two hours Peter and Lauren had welcomed Cameron into their home. Beyond helping meet Cameron's most basic needs with a safe place to live and sufficient food to eat, Peter and Lauren became a support system for him. Soon, with Peter and Lauren's help, Cameron was going back to school to fulfill his desire to become a mechanic. He also started attending church, where Peter and Lauren introduced him to friends who have now become a stable (and enjoyable!) community around him.

The letter I hold in my hands is written to the church members who have become Cameron's friends—or actually, family. Cameron writes:

"Thank you for caring for me ... Sometimes I think to myself, where would I be [if it wasn't for the church] and honestly I am not sure I would still be alive ... Your help has been more than just help. It has been a second chance. A second chance to see the world for the good that is in it ... It has been like having the parent I was never able to have ... I just want to thank you for being there."

What if Christmas isn't just about having our own needs met but actually loving others enough to lay down our lives in service to them all throughout the year?

Needless to say, Cameron's Christmas this year is going to be much different than it would have been apart from people living the way Jesus showed us how to live.

What if Christmas isn't just about having our own needs met and longings fulfilled one time a year, but actually loving others enough to lay down our lives in service to them all throughout the year?

Left to ourselves, we'll never be able to love like this. But that actually leads us to the last reason Jesus came, and it's the most surprising of all.

Reason 4

To be
your servant

Reason 4

To be your servant

… but to serve …

Imagine for a moment going out for a special meal this Christmas season with a close friend or family member. Surrounded by nice Christmas décor, someone comes over to your table and looks at you with a genuine smile on his or her face, asking, "How can I serve you?"

With this picture in your mind, I encourage you to realize that this is Jesus' posture toward you. God in the flesh has come to you and said, "I am here to serve you."

This is the stunning reality of Mark 10:45 that I mentioned earlier. It's so shocking, I find it hard to process, let alone believe. But Jesus said, as clearly and plainly as possible, "The Son of Man came not to be served but *to serve*." Jesus uses this same word on another occasion to describe how in heaven, for all who have placed their trust in him, "he will dress himself for *service* and have them recline at table, and he will come and *serve* them" (Luke 12:37).

> Other religions are built around what you can do for God, not what God can do for you

Religious leaders don't talk or act like this. Other religions are built around what you can do for God, not what God can do for you. But Jesus did not come as a powerful leader whose personal whims would be catered to *by* lowly servants.

Instead, Jesus came to *be* the lowly servant. Of you and me. Doesn't this sound almost preposterous (if not blasphemous) to even say—that God works for us as our servant?

———

Now let's be clear about what Jesus *doesn't* mean when he calls himself our servant. He doesn't mean that we just tell him whatever we want him to do, and he automatically does it. Like a parent who is prepared to say "No" to their children, Jesus is too kind to cater to our every worldly desire like this.

In addition, the Bible says in many places that followers of Jesus are *his* servants. After all, he is God, which means he is Lord of our lives. The key to happiness is living according to the leadership of the one who created us, loves us, and knows what is best for us. But it's important to realize that Jesus doesn't *need* us to serve him. As God, he is completely self-sufficient and doesn't rely on us for anything. Instead, we need him.

And that's the point: Jesus is saying he wants to meet our deepest needs! Think about our deepest needs in light of what we have already explored. We have all sinned against God, and we all need God's forgiveness. Our greatest need in life is for God to remove the guilt and shame of our sin and restore us to relationship with him. For it's in relationship with God, who is the Giver of every good gift, that we can and will find every good thing we need.

But here's the problem: we can't meet our deepest needs on our own because we can't get to God on our own, no matter how hard we try. When I remember my friends outside the Southeast Asian temple saying we're all working our way up the mountain to God, I can't help but think about high Asian mountains that I've trekked in the past. It's not uncommon to be walking up a steep incline and think you're almost to the top. You press on through the pain, believing you're about to arrive when finally you crest the incline and realize (with much disappointment and exhaustion) that it was a false summit. In reality, you still have so much further to go, in ways you couldn't see from where you were previously standing.

Religion is filled with false summits like this—with people thinking that if I just pray a certain amount, or do enough good deeds, or attend enough religious services, then I will be okay. But the reality is, no matter how hard we try, we can't erase the stain of sin on our hearts before God. This means that the path to reconciliation with God can't actually be paved by serving God. Instead, you and I need God to serve us. And that's why Jesus is saying, "I came *to serve* you, not to *be served* by you."

If you have never asked God to serve you in this way, I invite you to do that right now. This is the most important decision you could ever make in your life, for this is the only way to be forgiven of your sin, to be restored to relationship with God, and to receive eternal life with him. In this moment, I invite you to pause and pray something like this:

> *"God, I know that I have sinned against you, and I need you to serve me. I believe that Jesus came to live the life I couldn't live, to die the death I deserve to die, and to conquer the enemy I cannot conquer— death itself. Today, I want to turn from my sin and trust in Jesus as the Savior and Lord who gave his life to ransom me. Please forgive me of my sin and restore me to relationship with you for all of eternity."*

This is a prayer God promises to answer in your life. This is the moment God is longing for you to come to. God desires to serve you by meeting your greatest need now and forever—if you will ask and trust him to do so.

I remember when my wife and I brought home our first newborn child one December just before Christmas. We had no idea what to do with this little baby boy. When do we feed him? When does he sleep? How do we get him to sleep? How do we stop him from crying?

I distinctly recall the first bath we gave him in the little tub we had. We actually pulled up the step-by-step instructions the hospital had given us for bathing a newborn.

First, wet the rag. We did it.

Second, put a dab of organic, tear-free, alcohol-free baby soap on the rag. Okay, check. Now what?

Meanwhile, as we're looking at the instructions, our poor baby was screaming because he was freezing cold. I could just see him thinking to himself, "Why did I get stuck with the rookies? They have no clue what they're doing!"

We learned pretty quickly. We had to because this baby boy was completely dependent on us. Without being served, a baby cannot live.

I share this illustration because it reminds me of some words Jesus told his followers:

> *"... whoever does not receive the kingdom of God like a child shall not enter it."* (Mark 10:15)

Childlike faith is at the heart of following Jesus, and it hinges on realizing our total dependence on him. Jesus did not come to the world in search of servants who would cater to his needs. Instead, he came in search of people who would humble themselves before God like a child in a mother's or father's arms, acknowledge their need for him to serve them, and receive his sacrificial love for them. And not just for a short time, but for their entire lives.

Childlike faith is at the heart of following Jesus

Think about how everything in Christianity depends on God serving his people. For example, prayer is saying to God, "I'm going through this challenge, and I need you to help me." Even praying for others is saying, "God, this person is in a difficult situation, and they need you." God has invited us to pray to him in every circumstance about everything we need, confident that he will serve us by answering our prayers according to his power, wisdom, and love.

This carries over into every facet of our lives. I think about all the ways I need God in the course of a normal day. I need strength from God to even get out of bed. I need to listen to God's Word every morning in order to reframe my perspective on what matters most in the world. As I do my job, I need God's strength to work hard and wisely for my and others' good. All throughout the day, I need God for all the fruit that flows from him: love, joy, peace, patience, kindness, goodness, faithfulness, gentleness, and self-control (Galatians 5:22–23). I need God all day long to save me from sin and selfishness, to help me love and serve others, and to satisfy my often restless, anxious soul through trust in him as I lay my head on my pillow at night. And the beauty is: God promises to provide for all of my needs in all of these ways and more!

――――――

At this point, some people might say, "This is the problem with Christianity. It's for the weak. Christianity is for those who need a crutch because they can't do it on their own." Some people might even think, "I don't need God to serve me. I get up early every morning. I work hard all day. I get along with my life just fine, doing all kinds of good things."

I don't doubt that these people work hard and do good to others. But it's worth asking: Where do you get the breath to wake up in the morning?

Where does the food and water come from that gets you through your day? Who made your body and mind, allowing you to work?

The reality is, not one person in the world is truly self-sufficient. Every person in the world—including you—is God-dependent. Even if you hate the idea of God, the reality is that your ability to think this thought comes from the very one you hate.

Every one of us needs God. A relationship with God begins by realizing this. Then that relationship continues day by day and moment by moment with this realization.

And the good news of Christmas is that Jesus is a servant who came to supply all that you need.

Conclusion

What do you
want for
Christmas?

Conclusion

What do you want for Christmas?

We started this journey by pausing and asking the question: If you could receive anything for Christmas, what would it be? As we answered that question, I assume our minds went in a variety of different directions. But whatever came to your mind, my hope is that now, at the end of this journey, you have fresh perspective on how the heart of Christmas is God's desire to meet our deepest needs and fulfill our ultimate desires.

Christmas is not just a celebration of gifts we might give or receive in this world; it's a declaration that the God who created this world has come to us in Jesus to serve us, to save us from our sins, and to satisfy our souls for all of eternity, starting right now. The monumental truth of Christmas is that Jesus—God in the flesh—offers to serve you in every way you need amidst everything you face in this world.

> The God who created this world has come to us in Jesus to satisfy our souls

Just think about various struggles you experience in life and sometimes feel even more acutely at Christmas. No matter what you may face, Jesus wants to give you what you most need in that situation.

In your struggles with fear and insecurity,
Jesus wants to give you freedom and refuge.
(Psalm 46:1-3)

In your struggles with worry and anxiety,
Jesus wants to give you confidence and peace.
(Philippians 4:5-7)

In your struggles with depression and despair,
Jesus wants to give you faith and hope.
(Romans 5:1-5)

In your struggles with loneliness and weakness,
Jesus wants to give you his presence
and strength.
(Philippians 4:13, 19)

In your struggles with grief and sorrow,
Jesus wants to give you comfort and joy.
(2 Corinthians 1:3-11)

In your struggles with pride and selfishness,
Jesus wants to give you humility and selflessness.
(Philippians 2:1-11)

In your struggles with guilt and sin, Jesus
wants to give you forgiveness and restoration.
(Romans 8:1-39)

When we turn from sin and commit our lives to him, Jesus shares with us his wisdom, kindness, healing, courage … I could keep going, but that's kind of the point. In every struggle we have in our lives and every situation we experience in this world, Jesus is saying, "I am here for you."

Then one day, you and I are going to take our last breath. It could be many days from now or it could be today for any one of us. We don't know when that day will be, but if you have trusted in Jesus as your Savior and Lord, you can be confident of this: in that moment your body stops breathing, the one who came to conquer death will be right there with you, as he ushers you into eternal life with him.

———

As I get closer to Christmas, I'm spending a lot of time thinking about what family members and friends might like for a gift, and how I might be able to find and get them something they want. If I'm honest, this whole process can be mentally stressful! But do you know what brings my mind indescribable peace, and not just in the Christmas season? It's knowing that God—the Creator and Sustainer of everything that exists—is committed to me in every way. He promises the same to you, if you'll turn to him as your Lord and Savior.

This is why Jesus came: to be with you, to die instead of you, to show you how to live, and to be your servant. I encourage you to decide today to let him do all that he came to do for you. I encourage you to lay aside any and all of your pride, turn from your sin and yourself, and trust him to give you what you most want and need not just this Christmas, but all throughout the year and for all of eternity.

More books from 10Publishing

Resources that point to Jesus